Old Soldier Never Dies
(A Play)

Written by
Austyeno Babyeno

Devcom

All rights reserved.

Old Soldier Never Dies: A Play
© Austyeno Babyeno
Email: austyeno@hotmail.com

ISBN 978-0-9935237-9-3

First Published as Regimental Strife in April 2003 by Royal Pace Publications, Agbor, Nigeria.
Revised and republished in January 2025

Published by Devcom Media, Jersey, CI, United Kingdom

No part of this publication may be reproduced, stored in a retrieval system, or transmitted in any form, or by any means (electronic, mechanical, photocopying, recording, or otherwise, or be circulated in any form of binding or cover other than that in which it is published without the prior written permission of the publisher. A similar condition is being imposed on the subsequent purchaser.

British Library Cataloguing in Publication Data
A record for this book is available from the British Library.

Reader's Discretion Advised
This literary piece is characterised by satirical and improbable situations. The expressions and characters are purely fictional.

Page formatting: Austen Uwosomah
Copy Editing: Kennedy Edegbe
Cover monument photo: Adaku Chibuike.
Cover design: Matthew Godwin

If you take a moment to review our country's past, you would appreciate its present situation and could then anticipate what's waiting in the pipeline. The future of everyone will end the day they die, but not their country's.

*Dedicated
to the future of
Our beloved country.*

Contents

Dramatis Personae   VI
scene One   1
Scene Two   10
Scene Three 36
Scene Four   41
Scene Five   60
Scene Six   72
Glossary   85

Dramatis Personae

Mr President   (His Excellency)
Minister of Defence   (Dagogo)
Chief of Army Staff
CHIEF OF NAVAL STAFF
CHIEF OF AIR STAFF
Inspector General of Police   (Gambo)
Ben Loco
Bigler
Tiko
Amadi
Osadebe
Akpobi
Chima
Opara   (Osadebe's son)
Ceremonial Soldiers   (Opara and six others,)
Commandant   (Parade leader)
Superintendent
Policemen   (four of them)
Military Band (six of them)
Clergy Men   (Two of them)
Iman
Chief of Defence Staff
Executive Cabinet Members (Vice   President,   Senate President, House of Rep Speaker, etc)
Other Guests   (Invitees and foreign visitors)

scene One

[*The scene opens in the executive president's office which is tastefully furnished with state-of-the-art furniture. A green-white-green flag props behind the president's executive chair. The coat of arms and the president's portrait are visible on the wall. His Excellency himself is sitting in his chair, wearing a marigold embroidered white Agbada and a matching cap, grimly reading a petition letter. There are four other men sitting in the office too. One of the men Dagogo (the executive Minister of Defence) is in a grey-embroidered white Agbada. The other three men (the chiefs of staff of the navy, the army and the air force) clad in heraldic pristine military uniforms. Four of them sit in silence. The President finishes and straightens up*]

PRESIDENT: My dear chiefs of staff, I quite understand the grievance of this petition. I apologise for the way my predecessors had neglected the welfare of the army. I assure you that arrangements will be put in place soon to better the situation.

MINISTER OF DEFENCE: Permission to speak freely Your Excellency.

PRESIDENT: You may do so, Dagogo.

MINISTER OF DEFENCE: Thank you, Your Excellency. I like to add that it was due to the manner the last administration overlooked the welfare of our military.

PRESIDENT: What went wrong that they didn't care?

CHIEF OF ARMY STAFF: Your Excellency, I would say the obvious reason was to punish the military for latching on to power for a prolonged time.

PRESIDENT: Is that so?

CHIEF OF ARMY STAFF: I think so, your Excellency.

PRESIDENT: But why did you decide to latch on to the reigns for so long?

CHIEF OF NAVAL STAFF: We were not part of the junta your Excellency.

CHIEF OF ARMY STAFF: That's true your excellency, we weren't involved at all.

CHIEF OF AIR STAFF: Your excellency, we were confined to the barracks and didn't participate in the previous military regimes.

PRESIDENT: Of course I know that. You *(Points to the uniformed men)* are lucky you were not part of it, otherwise I wouldn't have appointed you to work in my administration.

CHIEF OF ARMY STAFF: We quite understand, your Excellency. We are grateful.

CHIEF OF NAVAL STAFF: It's a privilege to work with you, your Excellency.

CHIEF OF AIR STAFF: The same applies to me your Excellency.

PRESIDENT: Very well my service chiefs. I am delighted to hear that. Just keep it that way.

CHIEF OF ARMY STAFF: Your Excellency, you can rest assure I pledge my full support for democracy.

CHIEF OF NAVAL STAFF: Your Excellency, I also pledge to support democracy too.

CHIEF OF AIR STAFF: Your Excellency, To support what my colleagues have rightly said, you can count on us to defend democracy in our country, going forward.

PRESIDENT: You've all spoken well. I am glad you are inclined to let democracy reign in our country this time around. As for the complaints here (*Taps on the papers*) I assure you that my administration will have it sorted. Going forward, we shall prioritize the welfare of the army, most especially the aspect of professionalisation. The rank and file, who are due for promotion, will be promoted. All allowances owed to them by the previous government will be paid in full. In addition, the barracks around the country that lack amenities will be provided with the facilities. Where any is found to be in a bad state, it will be repaired. Give my apologies to your staff, and tell them to rescind their proposed strike action. You must remind them of their pledge to uphold the unity of our country and defend it at all times. The army cannot be unpatriotic no matter what. I am counting on you to make sure they refrain from their proposed strike. Do you understand me?

THE MILITARY CHIEFS: *(All together)* Yes, your Excellency!!!

PRESIDENT: Very good.

MINISTER OF DEFENCE: Let me add that the President is right. The strike is uncalled for, so must be averted. You have to make sure of that.

THE MILITARY CHIEFS: *(All together)* Yes!!!

PRESIDENT: That will be all for now. You may take your leave, service chiefs.

[*The military chiefs stand and each demonstrates a soldier's salute to the President. They also salute Dagogo and thereafter walk off. The president waits for them to leave and then gathers the papers before turning to Dagogo*]

PRESIDENT: *(Hands* Dagogo *the papers)* Keep these in your custody. Take charge and facilitate the promises I made. Take note of the areas I noted and fix them accordingly. Okay?

MINISTER OF DEFENCE: *(Receiving the papers)* Yes, your Excellency."

Come to think of it, Dagogo, how did it get so bad that the past administration neglected the military's welfare?

MINISTER OF DEFENCE: Your Excellency, it's my opinion that the last administration deliberately cut off funding to the army to punish the organ for latching on to power, and also for their misrule of our country's resources.

PRESIDENT: That is understandable. I hate to think the khaki wearers thought they could be better administrators than us.

MINISTER OF DEFENCE: It still baffles me your Excellency.

PRESIDENT: Who would have thought our army will purport a Strike Action? They want to join other workers who are on strike to press home their demands. The rate at which our parastatals are indulging in strike action is alarming. I have not been in office for up to a year, and some of our parastatals have either gone on strike, or are gunning to go, like my administration was responsible for the economic decadence that has affected the country.

MINISTER OF DEFENCE: your Excellency, there has been one strike action too many. The sectors are just capitalising on it these days. I would not have imagined the Army would plan to do same.

PRESIDENT: The act is the new normal. I didn't believe it when ASUU, ASUP and the teachers union went on strike to cripple the academic system. Then the doctors and the nurses also did that to the medical field too. Not to talk of the havoc which the NUPENG's industrial action brought upon the petroleum market.

MINISTER OF DEFENCE: your Excellency, I find it all puzzling. But the one that baffled me the most was the strike action of the medical practitioners who thought money was more important than saving lives.

PRESIDENT: Theirs was a shameful unethical behaviour. Callousness to the sick is against their work ethics.

MINISTER OF DEFENCE: your Excellency, in my opinion, I think the planned strike of the Police force was the most ignoble of all.

PRESIDENT: Don't even remind me about that. Who would have thought the police force of a country would ever plan to embark on Strike?

MINISTER OF DEFENCE: Your Excellency, that would have been the highest sabotage of them all.

Should the police have withdrawn the security they provided, that would have created a field day for robbers and urchins to our detriment, and we wouldn't have been able to move about safely.

PRESIDENT: Of course. Theirs would have been a gross irresponsible act. police strike isn't justifiable in any way, because it is against police code of conduct.

MINISTER OF DEFENCE: Your Excellency, you did well to timely stop that proposed police strike. You averted the breakdown of law and order, and possible chaos.

PRESIDENT: I know. That's why I dealt decisively with the arrowheads who spear headed the unpatriotic act. The idiots will remain dismissed from the force until their dying day. That will teach them a lesson.

MINISTER OF DEFENCE: It served them right, they will know better next time.

PRESIDENT: It's important that I stop the proposed strike of the army too. The Armed Forces Remembrance Day is just around the corner. A lot of money will be dished out in preparation for the celebration. Besides, we have invited some foreign dignitaries from other countries to grace the occasion. Should the army refuses to perform the ceremony, that will disgrace our nation before the international eyes. I will not allow that.

MINISTER OF DEFENCE: You've said it all, Your Excellency. We shall meet the demands of the army so they don't have a cause to embarrass our country.

PRESIDENT: The one I don't like at all, is that our soldiers serving in Peacekeeping Missions abroad have also threatened to boycott the operations in solidarity with their colleagues at home. That will be a disgraceful thing in the eyes of the international community. Our country might lose its international credibility.

MINISTER OF DEFENCE: Your Excellency, May I also add that will be a big slap on our country's integrity. Not only that, it will slight our country's prestige and lower our military value. Our soldiers might not be allowed to participate in future international wars… er, I mean Peacekeeping operations.

PRESIDENT: That's why I must meet the demands of the military to avert that kind of embarrassment to our country.

MINISTER OF DEFENCE: That will be the wisest thing to do, your Excellency.

PRESIDENT: I shall instruct the Finance Minister to immediately release funds from the Federation Account to your ministry. You and the Minister for Works and Social Amenities should ensure the Army staff are paid their salaries up to date. Where amenities are lacking in their barracks, they should be fixed or provided. However, I would like you to concentrate more on the barracks of the lower ranks. I trust that you will be on top of the supervision of the whole exercise. Can I trust you to be in charge?

MINISTER OF DEFENCE: You can count on me to deliver on any assignments you give to me, your Excellency.

PRESIDENT: I know that. You have been loyal, Dagogo. I can rely on you any day.

MINISTER OF DEFENCE: *(Smiling like a humble puppet)* Thank you, your Excellency. I am glad you find my services very worthy.

PRESIDENT: It's okay Dagogo, you may leave now. I want to hear progress reports on your work soon.

MINISTER OF DEFENCE: *(Stands)* Very well, your Excellency. I shall do as you have directed. *(Picks a briefcase from his side and tucks the papers inside, then looks at the president)* Permission to take my leave Sir.

PRESIDENT: Alright Dagogo, goodbye.

MINISTER OF DEFENCE: Goodbye Sir *(Exits)*

LIGHT FADES

Scene Two

[*The scene opens at night time. In the dim light, silhouettes of five human figures at the front of an office building are vaguely visible. A beam of spot light comes on and shines on the shadowy figures one after the other. Two men are sitting astride on a bench, another two men are sitting back-to-back on a separate bench whilst the fifth man is lying supine on a mat. One of the men on the first bench lets out a thick cough, the other one beside him sneezes, the third man on the second bench grunts, the fourth man beside him yawns noisily whilst the sleeping man on the mat snores away.*

The spotlight goes off suddenly, followed by a sudden blast of floodlights that light up the scene. The bright lights reveal each man has his own walking stick lying on the ground beside him. The men are retired army pensioners waiting in front of an office. MILITARY PENSION BUREAU is inscribed on the signboard Above the office door. The sleeping man carries on snoring unaware of the change from night to morning. The other men stare at him mirthfully and talk about him]

BEN LOCO: *(Looking at the sleeping man)* Osadebe certainly knows how to sleep, doesn't he?

BIGLER: No doubt about that. I'm sure he' still suffers from that sting he got from a tsetse fly when he was a kid.

TIKO: That's impossible! The man is 73 years old and you say he is still suffering from a childhood disease?

AMADI: I don't believe you, Bigler. I know that Osadebe there *(points at the snoring man)* had fought in inter-continental wars. He was among the contingent who were drafted to Burma. He could not have done that if he had sleeping sickness.

TIKO: Point of correction Amadi, Burma is currently called Myanmar.

AMADI: Since when?

Bigler: It's true, Amadi. Burma is called Myanmar now.

AMADI: Myanmar doesn't sound better than Burma to me. I prefer to call it Burma, period!

Bigler: You can choose to be ignorant if you like. That's your cup of tea. Going back to what I was saying, Osadebe is from Ama Ijiji. That Village is a breeding ground for tsetse flies.

BEN LOCO: But that was a long time ago, Bigler. I can't remember the last time I heard about tsetse flies biting people in our country.

Bigler: You may be right. But Ama Ijiji was a habitat for tsetse flies when the place was still a bush hamlet. Even though the village has long developed and benefit from pipe-borne water and electricity, plus a general hospital, that doesn't mean there aren't one or two tsetse flies still flying about there.

AMADI: Excuse me Bigler, you are not right about the pipe-borne water and electricity.

BIGLER: I'm not wrong! My late wife was from Ama Ijiji' and I have been there many times so I am sure of what I said.

AMADI: Ama Ijiji' is not far from my own village, I have been there too. It is true that the Government provided them water and electricity, but that didn't last. Most of the electrical installations are no longer functioning. Their transformers were overloaded and only supplied epileptic power before they kaput one after the other. As for the pipe-borne water, the pipes which were burrowed in the ground to distribute water, all got rusted from lack of use. The people there depend on artificially sunk boreholes for water and petrol generators for electricity.

BIGLER: *(Nodding in assent)* You have truly been to the place. What you said is true. The people there are crazy about generators. I saw the smallest generator in my life the last time I was there. It was like the size of a flat screen TV and it—

BEN LOCO: *(Interrupts)Don't* start with yarning opata now, Bigler. That couldn't have been a generator you saw.

AMADI: Ever knowing and ever seeing Bigler, softly-softly spill your telltales here!

TIKO: Bigler, maybe what you saw was a solar panel.

BIGLER: *(Looks at them with a hurt expression)* So you think I don't know what I saw? You don't believe me?

BEN LOCO: Who said we don't? we believe you very much. If you had heard a voice telling you so, then it must be the voice of your conscience. Or comrades *(Looks at the others and bribes them with a wink)* did any of you say you didn't believe him?

COMRADES: No O!!!! *(They chorus and burst out laughing at BIGLER)*

BIGLER: You are laughing like jackasses and laughing at yourselves not me! You old men don't know anything. Osadebe would have confirmed what I said if he was awake. *(Looks at the sleeping man)* You can ask him when he wakes. He will verify what I said.

OSADEBE: *(Talks in his sleep)* Don't mind them, Bigler. It's because they do not know that the generator you are talking about is inside your bag. Why not take it out for all to see. Seeing is believing.

[*The comrades look at Bigler expectantly*]

BIGLER: *(Looking cowed and eyeing Osadebe mischievously)* It's like Osadebe also suffers from somniloquism.

AMADI: Bigler, Osadebe is fine. Just stop blowing your opata balloon here or it will burst in your face. If you have nothing better to say, just shh… Shh… Shh… Atishoo! Atishoo! Atishoo! Atishoo! *(Sneezes on)*

BIGLER: Aha! Old Boy, so you couldn't even finish your sentence before your nose starts itching for its food? Better feed it now before you sneeze to death.

AMADI: Atishoo! Ex… ex… excuse me comrades. I need to attend to an urgent business.

[*Amadi takes out a flat snuffbox from his breast pocket. Holding it in his left palm, he taps it with the elbow of his other hand, then with his palm and opens it. He pinches a tiny bit with his thumb and index finger and inhales the substance through one nostril whilst blocking the other with his middle finger. Osadebe suddenly sits up and stretches out his palm. Amadi gives Osadebe the snuffbox and he parody's Amadi's snuffing antics before putting some snuff into his own nostril*]

BEN LOCO: You old gargoyles can't just do without a bit of snuff, huh? How can you be snorting raw tobacco like that? Only the devil knows how much damage it would have done to your brains by now. I prefer refined tobacco with added menthol, like this brand. *(Fishes a pack of Marlborough out of his pocket and shows it)* These come with a cool minty flavour that blend with nicotine. The taste is pleasant, not like that crude snuff that might contain only God knows what. If one were to observe inside that snuffbox with a microscope, one might find some dreadful organisms living on the tobacco.

BIGLER: Tobacco is tobacco, be it refined or granulated. None is any good!

AMADI: Bigler, don't say what you don't know. Have you ever heard that snuff taking is dangerous to health, or did you hear anyone propound snuff takers are liable to die young?

OSADEBE: The answer is capital no! The only slogans I have heard on radio are the ones that prophesy doom for cigarette smokers. Some of them even carry predictions of serious health harms.

AMADI: Very correct! The summary of all the caution jingles is smokers have only but a short time to live, and that applies to you Ben. You are going to die early.

BEN LOCO: Me! Die early? Never mind the extreme propagandas of those jingoes. I believe it was one Surgeon General or so with the Federal Ministry of Health that endorsed them to warn smokers of early death. But he got it wrong absolutely! Let me tell you why! *(Stands)* Look at me, I am over 70 years old and still an active smoker. I started hearing the warning slogans on cigarette adverts on the mass media a long time ago before they stopped advertising cigarette completely. They used all sorts of gimmick to fine-tune the warnings. Smokers are liable to die young, smoking Is Dangerous To Health, it causes lung cancer, it can cause heart failure… blah-blah-blah. I have been smoking since I was nineteen, that's over fifty years. Look at me now, I am old and still a heavy smoker. If for any reason I drop dead now, will anybody say I died young?

BIGLER: I will certainly say so!

BEN LOCO: I beg your pardon? *(Looks at Bigler in surprise)*

BIGLER: Certainly! You are a walking corpse. That whooping cough you have is from tobacco excess. I doubt if your lungs and heart will come out clean in a CT scan. They must be as black as charcoal by now. No one will agree to accept them for organ replacement.

BEN LOCO: You are so wrong. My cough is nothing serious. It has nothing to do with Tobacco. It is just caused by a minor diplococci irritation I feel in my respiratory tract every now and then, otherwise I breathe fine. I don't have a congested chest. My lungs and heart are in ace condition. They will pass perfectly.

TIKO: Don't you try to confuse us with that medical jargon. I still think you should quit smoking all the same. You should be taking it easy at your age.

BEN LOCO: Pipe down, Tiko, you are the youngest here. You can't advise me. You are still a young man by our standards. You are the last one to retire from the army among us here. You'd only fought around Africa, under Britain's West African Frontier Force, and in the Civil War. Do you know what it was like during World War II when we were drafted to fight the Germans in faraway Scandinavia? The arctic breeze was always fanning at our chests and trying to freeze our lungs, even with our thermal jerkins on. We had to smoke cigarettes to keep our longs warm. No day went past that a soldier in my platoon didn't smoke a minimum of ten sticks. Thanks to our oyinbo leaders who shared packets of their foreign cigarillo to us in good quantities. That was when I tasted refined cigarettes for the first time. They saved me from the cold, but I also enjoyed puffing them too. I would give anything to relive those days again.

TIKO: Ben Loco, you are incorrigible. You are going to die if you keep smoking.

AMADI: Ben's days are numbered. He is only waiting to collect his pension first. I am sure when he gets the money he will use it to import a containerful of cigarettes and smoke himself to his grave.

BEN LOCO: And what will you do with your own money? This is my theory. You will start a tobacco grinding factory and keep all the snuff you produced for yourself. Then you will invite Osadebe over to share the produce with you. The two of you will have enough snuff to fertilise your arid nostrils. No wonder your eyes are always red. If snuffing was really great, why are your eyes bloodshot all the time like a fresh bullet wound? I bet they could cause convulsion in little children who stare into them. You have to cover them whenever children come your way to avoid incurring the wrath of their mothers.

AMADI: I think Ben Loco might already be dead. This person here might be his zombie. And the zombie is not even aware that the oyinbo who invented the cigarette also describes it as coffin nail.

BEN LOCO: Is it not the oyinbo that invented cigarette that also taught me to smoke it? Now, the same oyinbo turns around to warn me it will kill me? Who are they kidding? Why did they invent it in the first place?

AMADI: Have you gone gaga, Ben! Who are you asking those senseless questions? Do you see any oyinbo here? It appears your stay on earth is overdue. What you need now is a nice thorny coffin to lay your old bones in. Why not find yourself one and quietly yamutu inside so you can rest in peace.

BEN LOCO: Don't worry, old man, I will die eventually, but not before I have collected my pension. I won't leave that for the government. I will not let them deprive me of my entitlement because after serving in the army for many years, risking my life defending our country, the least the government can do is to sustain me in my old age. Anyone who thinks I will die before I collect every naira of my pension I am owed has another think coming. The government owes me two years in arrears so that's not small money. I need my money paid to the last naira so I can give it to my children to celebrate my burial after I kick the bucket.

OSADEBE: Yours is a good after death plan, Ben. But I doubt you will get a naira of your pension from this government.

TIKO: What do you mean, Osadebe? Are you saying that Ben Loco will not be paid his pension?

OSADEBE: Yes, not only he, but we as well.

TIKO: Are you insinuating that we will not be paid our pensions today? *(Looks at Osadebe searchingly)*

OSADEBE: Not that I wish they not pay us, but to be candid, I don't think the government is interested in paying us our pensions.

BEN LOCO: *(Stands to his feet with a bellicose look)* They had better be O, cos I won't take that nonsense!

OSADEBE: I doubt that very much.

BIGLER: Osadebe, what makes you say that?

OSADEBE: In case you didn't know, the serving military men were not paid their salaries for six months. Besides that, the rank and file has remained stagnant for several years with no promotion. I know from history that politicians don't have any sympathy for the military, this present government is no different.

BIGLER: That's not true. Our government recently settled the military.

OSADEBE: Yes, I know that. Our Government only decided to settle them in a hurry because they had wanted to embark on industrial action.

TIKO: *(Interrupts)* Point of correction, Osadebe. The military doesn't embark on industrial action. Rather, they go on strike.

OSADEBE: It is the same thing!

TIKO: No it's not!

BIGLER: Tiko, there's no difference between industrial Action and strike action. Please allow Osadebe to finish what he was saying.

TIKO: But it's not the same thing. Let me prove my point.

AMADI: I don't know what you want to prove. Be quiet and allow Osadebe to finish.

TIKO: You will get it clearly. Let me explain their differences. Industrial action is—

AMADI: *(Interrupts)* Shut up Tiko and let Osadebe carry on.

TIKO: How dare you, Amadi?

AMADI: Shut up my friend! Keep your bookish knowledge to yourself and let Osadebe talk.

TIKO: You must be very foolish to say that! I am trying to say what I know and you are shutting me up? I don't blame you for your ignorance. Anyway, comrades, let me explain it to—

AMADI: *(Interrupts again)* Shut up Tiko, or I will seal your mouth with glue!

TIKO: *(Raises his voice)* How dare you?

AMADI: *(Shouting)* For your own good, you'd better shut that cave you speak with now or I'll roll a rock over it!

TIKO: Just because you are older than me doesn't give you the audacity to belittle me. Do you even see yourself? You look like a dried Okporoko with your wizened long neck!

AMADI: *(Feels his neck with both hands in disbelief)* Who are you calling Okporoko?

TIKO: You, old gargoyle. Who do you think you are?

AMADI: You are a fucking arsehole!

TIKO: Your anatomy resembles the antiquated figure of a giraffe, with your tiny limbs and long neck!

AMADI: What did you say? You bombastic boorish buffoon!

TIKO: You are a good-for-nothing ignoramus!

BEN LOCO: That's enough! The two of you should… *(Breaks off and starts coughing)* Kpooh-ooh! Kpooh-ooh! Kpooh-ooh! Kpooh-ooh! Kpooh-ooh! Kpooh-ooh …

[*Ben Loco carries on coughing for a while. The other men look at him with concern shaking their heads pitifully. Ben manages to pull himself together and resumes talking*]

BEN LOCO: Sorry, comrades. Don't mind my coughing. As I was saying, Amadi and Tiko you should not quarrel here. We have all come here to collect our pensions from the officials of this office *(Points at the sign board above the door)*. We must therefore stay together in camaraderie.

BIGLER: Ben is right. Please Amadi and Tiko, desist from further confrontations.

AMADI: All right. Sorry for slighting you, Tiko.

TIKO: It's okay, Comrade Amadi. I withdraw my insults.

OSADEBE: Now that order has been restored, let me continue what I was saying. Our serving Army were contemplating to embark on industrial action, or go on strike *(Steals a glance at Tiko),* whichever you may choose to call it. The soldiers threatened they would not partake in the Armed Forces Remembrance Day Ceremony. Because of that, the government quickly settled the serving army so as to stop them from boycotting the Remembrance Day Ceremony.

[*The comrades look at Osadebe disbelievingly*]

BEN LOCO: How do you know all that?

OSADEBE: Through my son Opara, who joined the army eight years ago. He came to the village last week to see me. Actually, it was he that informed me about the commencement of pensions to ex-service soldiers. I have more gist if you want to know.

COMRADES: Tell us!!!!!

OSADEBE: Okay, all of you listen now. My son Opara has recently been promoted to the rank of sergeant, and has moved from his one-bedroom apartment at ECOMOG Barracks to a two-bedroom. He told me that Government paid all their arrears, promoted the rank and file, and also fixed the amenities in the barracks across the country.

BIGLER: If our Government has settled the serving soldiers, then there should be no problem settling the ex-service soldiers. Ours should follow suit.

OSADEBE: You don't understand. Our government hastily settled the serving soldiers because they threatened to go on strike. Have you not been following what is happening in the country? Let me enlighten you more. A few months back, the petroleum workers in charge of transporting crude oil had wanted to go on strike, but our government quickly met their demands. Also, the police had wanted to go on strike too but government met their demands as well. So, when the army threatened to do likewise, government promptly met their demands too. However, do you know that the academic staff of universities and the health practitioners in government hospitals are still on strike? Despite that they went on strike first, they are yet to receive any attention from government.

BEN LOCO: I don't understand. How does all that relate to us?

OSADEBE: It means that our government only acts if they have something to lose. Especially something that will cause an embarrassment.

AMADI: What do you mean?

OSADEBE: I will give you an example. The peacekeeping soldiers serving abroad threatened to boycott thee operations if the government didn't hearken to the demands of their colleagues at home. That would have embarrassed our government, so they averted it.

TIKO: So, you mean government only decided to meet the demands of the serving soldiers to avoid embarrassment?

OSADEBE: That is the bitter truth!

TIKO: That's not good, "Wallahi!

AMADI: Chaii! Goat has eaten palm leaf off my head!

BIGLER: Oghene biko, may it not be so O!

BEN LOCO: But the announcement clearly said they will commence payment of pensions to the retired soldiers today. That's why we are here, isn't it?

OSADEBE: No, that wasn't what was said in the news. The news said today is the last day of payment. They have been paying before now.

BEN LOCO: It doesn't look like anybody is coming to open this office today, does it? We were here before daybreak and are still waiting.

OSADEBE: I doubt this door will open today. We shall find out soon enough.

AMADI: Don't be pessimistic, Osadebe.

BIGLER: You need to stay positive, Osadebe. Don't forecast doom.

BEN LOCO: That's right, Osadebe. Have hope.

TIKO: I am with Osadebe.

[*The others turn to look at him with raised brows*]

TIKO: Comrades, maybe Osadebe is right. From my understanding of what he told us, it seems obvious that Government only acted because the serving soldiers threatened to go on strike, and also because their peacekeeping colleagues threatened to down tools. Isn't that right, Osadebe?

OSADEBE: Hundred per sent!

TIKO: Comrades, do you get it now? Our Government didn't slack at all. They know what to do if they choose to work.

BIGLER: What are you insinuating?

OSADEBE: The obvious. The point is that we are just some old army retirees who need succour. We seek for compensation from Government for services rendered to our country. we were supposed to be chilling, taking it easy and basking in the ambience of geriatric care, but here we are, sitting in the heat of the day, sweaty, hungry and with smelling mouths still waiting patiently for the pension officials to come to work.

TIKO: None of us stay in this city. We came from our respective villages yesterday to sleep here so we can meet up with today's deadline.

OSADEBE: Initially, they were making the payments at the Military Pension Liaisons in the different state capitals, Then they ran out of the cheques and told the late comers to proceed to FCT for theirs. But what is the time now? *(looks up at the sun)* it is getting to ten o'clock and no one has come to work to open the office!

BEN LOCO: But those who were here previously, had received their cheques? So what's wrong now? Is it because it's the last day today they don't want to come to work, or have they also run out of the cheques?

AMADI: I hope not, otherwise the orange will harden like a kernel!

BIGLER: They should not try nonsense O, otherwise I go crack bottles here!

BEN LOCO: Kaii! I wish I'd come earlier. Maybe I would have collected my cheque like those pensioners who got theirs.

OSADEBE: We better start planning what else to do because even if we wait here all day, I don't think this office will open today, or even at all.

TIKO: Haba! Don't they have any regard for us?

BEN LOCO: Maybe we could also threaten to go on strike, huh?

TIKO: We can, if we have a leverage we could use.

BIGLER: We cannot threaten to go on strike like the others, our situation is different. We do not have anything to purport that will embarrass the government.

TIKO: Are you saying we are no better than toothless dogs?

OSADEBE: It is so, Tiko. We can only whine like puppies.

BEN LOCO: No, comrades. We can do more than that! There must be something we can do that will embarrass the government!

[*The other comrades look at Ben Loco in surprise*]

BIGLER: Such as what?

BEN LOCO: *(Stands pulling a hard-face)* I don't see why we can't march to Aso Rock Villa and block the entrance!

AMADI: Are you out of your mind? Sit down my friend and talk some sense, not that jazz you just said.

BIGLER: Don't be ridiculous, Ben Loco. I don't think that is a good idea. What you are suggesting is tantamount to civil disturbance. We will be apprehended and thrown into prison.

BEN LOCO: *(Sits)* They can't do that. We are in a democracy. Freedom to demonstrate is allowed.

BIGLER: But freedom to demonstrate does not mean we can obstruct the free passage of others, especially the free movements of the government officials who work at Aso Rock. Don't you know if we block the gates of Aso Rock it will prevent the officials who work there from going to carry out their national duties?

BEN LOCO: So what else can we do then?

OSADEBE: Nothing we can do but to sit here and wait for the pensions staff to come. So far so good, it doesn't look like that's going to happen. We might end up waiting here until the hen grows teeth.

AMADI: Chineke-meh! Goat has eaten palm leaf off my head!

BEN LOCO: So, we should just sit here and wait in vain? Is that it?

BIGLER: There must be something that we can do.

OSADEBE: There is nothing we can do. We are just like toothless dogs. Even if we bark from now till the sky falls, as long as we can't bite, no one will take us seriously, let alone pay us our money.

TIKO: I have an idea comrades! *(Stands and addresses them)* From my calculations, the sole reason why Government paid the serving army is to stop them boycotting the forthcoming Armed Forces Remembrance Day ceremony. So, let's do something about that.

BIGLER: Such as what?

TIKO: As a matter of fact, we are part of the heroes they will be paying tribute to on the day, isn't it?

BIGLER: No. The ones they will be honouring are our colleagues who died fighting along with us.

BEN LOCO: So, because we survived and didn't die in the battles, we don't deserve honour?

AMADI: It appears our government deems it better to spend money honouring the memory of dead heroes of war than to cater for the survivals. What with all that prodigal parade and gun-salute for dead soldiers?

TIKO: Not even one among the civilians in the current government fought alongside the dead heroes.

OSADEBE: The bloody civilians do not know the heroes, nor do the ceremonial zombies who will parade on the day to shoot the volley. Yet they are going to celebrate the dead heroes with a pageant ceremony, While we who knew them and fought by their sides have not been paid our pensions.

BEN LOCO: Some of those dead heroes were our pals who we fought side-by-side with. We returned alive from the wars, and our government don't value us? That's not fair!

BIGLER: It beats me that our government attaches more value to the fallen soldiers than they do to the living ex-service men. That's a typical example of our government's insensitivity to our plight.

TIKO: We should do something!

BIGLER: Such as what?

TIKO: I don't know. Are we not soldiers?

OSADEBE: We used to be, but not anymore. We are retired now. We are old and weak, and can easily be squashed like bread loaves.

BEN LOCO: I don't feel weak. I can't be squashed like a loaf of bread. Never mind I am old. I am still strong. *(Flexes his biceps and gesticulates wielding an assault rifle)* Give me a pump action now and I will show you my mojo.

TIKO: How about we show them an old soldier never dies?

BIGLER: That's right! We are the living heroes, old soldiers who survived the wars!

OSADEBE: The very gallant ones who went head-to-head against death and returned alive!

BEN LOCO: We escaped death and came back in tact!

BIGLER: If we didn't die or lose our members in the wars, what else can kill us?

AMADI: Nothing can kill me, even now. I still believe in my Odeshi!

TIKO: The fallen soldiers are not any more important than us. Why should the survivals of wars deserve less respect than the dead? Our government should accord us honour and treat us with dignity as well.

BIGLER: There's no sense in glorifying dead heroes who can't appreciate it. The dead don't count in war. Why waste money on their memories?

OSADEBE: I think it would be more realistic if government gives grants and scholarships to the widows and children of the dead soldiers every year, instead of lavishing money on the celebration of the Armed Forces Remembrance Day. Moreover, some veterans who returned physically disabled, shell-shocked, or with posttraumatic disorder, are in dire need of support. Would it not be better if government assists those needy veterans with disability allowances and mental support, instead of spending the money on gun-salute and wreaths in honour of dead soldiers?

AMADI: That's a sensible talk my friend. If only our government can have compassion for the needy, there will be less hardship for the unprivileged. But they prefer to spend money on pomp elephant projects, that's why they don't care about old soldiers like us.

BEN LOCO: I find the act of blowing a bugle to summon the souls of the fateful departed to the cenotaph post very ridiculous. And then they will go on to pretend their spirits are there and lay wreaths before firing twenty-one bullets. What a waste of ammunition!

BIGLER: The 21-gun salute tends to scare the birds away, that's pretty much all it does.

AMADI: I don't see how the dead soldiers who can't see or hear benefit from the extravagant ceremony. They don't really gain anything from it.

TIKO: The government benefits. The ceremony is just one of the magics they orchestrate to siphon our country's money. Imagine the idiots releasing white pigeons from their cage to glorify the dead heroes, whereas the dead have no clue of what's done in their honour. The ceremony is unproductive and just a flashy razmataz.

BEN LOCO: Our government should rather look after the living. Dead soldiers don't need food. Urgh… I am hungry to my bones. That makes me very angry!

OSADEBE: I totally get you brother. A hungry man is an angry man!

BEN LOCO: My anger has reached up to here *(Points to his throat)*. I am just so fed up with the system!

TIKO: I don't know about you comrades, but I am determined to fight for my right this time around!

BIGLER: I think we are too old to do gragra now O! We should exercise some patience and give the government some time!

TIKO: *(Stands up agilely)* No! Time waits for no one. time doesn't sit in a chair folding its hands and crossing its legs. My patience has been tried long enough. How can the government not pay me my pension for over six months? What do they want me to eat? Sand? The time has come to fight for my pension! It is now!

[*The comrades gaze at Tiko with concern. Tiko stares back at them with a hardened face. He then picks up his walking stick and stabs it into the air aggressively, challenging the others with a bellicose look*]

TIKO: Are you with me, comrades?

COMRADES: *(All quickly pick up their canes, hit them on Tiko's and simultaneously shout)* Old soldier never dies!!!!

LIGHT FADES

Scene Three

[*The scene opens in the President's office with His Excellency sitting in his chair. Sitting in the office too is a man (Gambo) clad in a pristine decorated police uniform with three stars and the insignia of inspector general. The president looks worried*]

PRESIDENT: Why for God's sake would those old soldiers want to disrupt the celebration of the Armed Forces Remembrance Day? Just when I thought I have everything under control, I am faced with another stumbling block. I have only just recently milked the federation account dry to settle the serving army, suddenly, the army retirees want to stir up their own trouble. What is wrong with the likes of soldiers and ex-soldiers in our country? It seems they are in a conspiracy to hinder the smooth running of my administration?

INSPECTOR GENERAL OF POLICE: It appears to be so, your Excellency.

PRESIDENT: Even you the police is not left out in the strike malady. Didn't the force threatened to strike back then? You people only think about reaping money from government.

INSPECTOR GENERAL OF POLICE: I am sorry your Excellency.

PRESIDENT: Don't tell me sorry. Will sorry solve the issue? Keep your srry to yourself.

INSPECTOR GENERAL OF POLICE: Sorry Sir… I mean okay Sir.

PRESIDENT: Something has obviously gone wrong with the labour force of our country. They are only interested in what our country will do for them, whereas it should've been the other way round. The public workers are using strike as modus operandi to press home their point. They have become like Oliver Twist, asking for more, like they don't understand my government had inherited the economic problems of our country. Do they expect me to fix all the problems in one year? How do they expect me to do that? Is my work a cut-and-nail job? Or Am I a magician?

INSPECTOR GENERAL OF POLICE: No, Sir.

PRESIDENT: I haven't yet figured how to settle the academic unions who are on strike, now the army pensioners want to start their own drama too? There is no money to pay their pensions. They need to exercise some patience and refrain from their silly idea. Disrupting the forthcoming Armed Forces Remembrance Day ceremony is not acceptable. The occasion will be broadcast on satellite to audiences around the world, so those ex-service men need to steer clear from the venue. Our country cannot afford the embarrassment they want to cause. You have to stop them, Gambo!

INSPECTOR GENERAL OF POLICE: *(Looks stunned)* Me? Your Excellency, No O!

PRESIDENT: *(Glares at him)* What do you mean by that?

INSPECTOR GENERAL OF POLICE: Your Excellency, those men are retired army officers O!

PRESIDENT: So what? Is it not your duty to ensure law and order?

INSPECTOR GENERAL OF POLICE: I am not sure if the police has the authority to arrest an ex-army. Maybe that falls under the jurisdiction of the military police. I will have to check with the Minister of Defence.

PRESIDENT: Are you not okay Gambo? I am telling you what you will do and you are talking about checking with the defence minister first? Did the minister give you your job?

INSPECTOR GENERAL OF POLICE: Pardon me, your Excellency. The ex-soldiers will be stopped if they try any nonsense there on that day. My men will round them up. I can assure you of that Sir.

PRESIDENT: Now you are talking like the Inspector General of Police. Now that you have understood why I sent for you, you must act accordingly. Make sure your men are on ground on the day to prevent the old soldiers from spoiling the ceremony.

INSPECTOR GENERAL OF POLICE: It will be done, Your Excellency. If the ex-service men dare show up on the grounds, they will be arrested and charged with federal terrorism.

PRESIDENT: That's good! In the meantime, I want you to place a police communiqué on the radio and TV to advise them not to break the law. Importantly, let the pensioners know that Government has put a plan in place to resume their pension payments soon. Apologise for the disappointment they experience at the pension offices. Let them know payments will resume again shortly, and that they will receive their pensions in full. Finally, emphasize justice will be served on them should they breech the laws of the land.

INSPECTOR GENERAL OF POLICE: All correct Sir. I will take care of it. But your Excellency, permit me to ask a question Sir.

PRESIDENT: What is it?

INSPECTOR GENERAL OF POLICE: Just to clarify things, do you mind if I ascertained from the Defence Minister if the police has powers to arrest ex-soldiers?

PRESIDENT: Why are you asking me a stupid question? Should I be the one to teach you how to do your job? If you don't know how to take care of dissident old army retirees, tender your resignation right now! I will appoint someone who can do the job without asking dumb questions.

INSPECTOR GENERAL OF POLICE: Pardon me, your Excellency. That was a slip of tongue. My men will be on the ready to squash the plans of the ex-service men if they show up at the arena. You can count on me.

PRESIDENT: Very good. That's the right attitude. You may leave now. Do your work. Put the necessary machineries in place.

INSPECTOR GENERAL OF POLICE: Yes sir. Permission to take my leave Sir.

PRESIDENT: Granted.

INSPECTOR GENERAL OF POLICE: Goodbye Sir! ()

[*The Inspector General stands and salutes the President who nods approvingly and watches him exits. The President sighs. He picks up a file from his desk and begins to go through the papers*]

LIGHT FADES

Scene Four

[*The scene opens on a grass field in the compound of a disused primary school which has some collapsed buildings. Stacks of cement blocks pile up in a corner nearby. Footfalls suddenly approach. Enter Osadebe and two men. Each man is carrying his own portable Ghana-must -go bag and mat. The men with Osadebe are Akpobi and Chima. Chima has a round cheerful face, although he is seemingly gaunt and hunched with age. Akpobi himself has a chubby tough-looking face and is endowed with a brawny muscular physique. The three lower their belongings on the ground and glance around the place. Akpobi whispers something to Chima who whispers back, then they carry on whispering between themselves. Osadebe moves aside and talks*]

OSADEBE: These men are my clansmen. They are ex-soldiers like me. We were conscripted into the infantry battalion of the Commonwealth Army to fight against the forces of Imperial Japan and India in the Second World War. They couldn't join us at the Pension Office last time because they didn't have money to pay their transport fares. I have brought them so they can participate in our planned demonstration. They themselves are eager to fight for their right too. But I have let them know what we intend to do isn't a warfare, but a peaceful march that will draw the attention of the world to our plight. *(Turns to the men and Calls)* Akpobi!

AKPOBI: *(Stamps one foot on the ground and demonstrates a soldier's salute)* Captain Armstrong Akpobi reporting to duty, Sir!

OSADEBE: Ah-ah? You don't need to do that. We are not observing rank here.

AKPOBI: *(Remains poised at attention)* Lieutenant Colonel Osadebe, Sir! Courtesy demands that. You were my senior in the Army!

[*OSADEBE ignores Akpobi and turns to the older man*]

OSADEBE: Chima?

CHIMA: *(Salutes like Akpobi)* Major Enoch Chima reporting to duty, Sir! *(Stays poised at attention too)*

OSADEBE: Chima, not You too. Cut it out please.

[*Chima doesn't shift. He remains stiff and straight-faced, standing at attention*]

OSADEBE: *(Salutes)* All right. Stand at ease both of you.

AKPOBI: I was wondering whether you have lost the soldier attitude.

CHIMA: I was thinking the same too. That's why I didn't budge till he complied.

OSADEBE: Not at all. Once a soldier, always a soldier.

[Enters Amadi, carrying his own bag and mat]

AMADI: Yes, comrades! Once a soldier, always a soldier! Greetings!

[The others turn to look at Amadi]

OSADEBE: Colonel Amadi is here!

AMADI: Greetings comrades!

[The comrades salute Amadi and remain poising at attention. AMADI Returns their salute and tells them to stand at ease]

AMADI: Where are the others?

OSADEBE: They will be here sooner or later.

CHIMA: Can we find somewhere to sit please? My leg is hurting. I can't keep standing for long.

AKPOBI: Where's your walking stick?

CHIMA: Oh! It got broken some days back when I used it to kill a snake that chased a rat into my house. But Tiko will be bringing me a new one today. Isn't that so, Osadebe?

OSADEBE: Oh yes. I asked Tiko to buy you one from his place as they are much cheaper there.

AKPOBI: Sorry for your loss Pa Chima.

CHIMA: What loss?

AKPOBI: Your third leg of course.

CHIMA: What can an old man with old legs do without a walking stick?

AKPOBI: If only you were as strong as me, you would not need one.

CHIMA: Don't you brag to me. You were just lucky to inherit the bone genes that runs in your paternal lineage.

OSADEBE: Chima, look over there! *(Points at the stacks of blocks)* if you would like to sit, we could use those as makeshift seats. We can carry some for our use.

CHIMA: *(looking towards where Osadebe is pointing)* Where are the seats? I can't see any.

AKPOBI: Pa Chima, look farther. Don't you have your glasses with you? Or did you break that too while you were killing the snake?

CHIMA: Don't be silly Akpobi. My glasses is only for reading. I don't use it for distance. *(Walks towards the pile of blocks)* Are you referring to those blocks, Osadebe?

AMADI: He means those, Chima. Let's help ourselves to some.

[*The men move towards the blocks. Each carries his own block and set back to where their bags are. Ben Loco and Bigler enter and greet the comrades. They observe the other comrades and set their bags down before going to get a block each. They all set their blocks upright and sit on them*]

CHIMA: These blocks come in very handy. They are really helpful.

AKPOBI: I think They will be used to build classrooms here to replace those ones that collapsed.

AMADI: It seems so.

OSADEBE: Comrades, now that Ben and Bigler are here, let's delve into the business at hand.

BEN LOCO: Why the hurry? Give me a break. I travelled a long way.

BIGLER: Osadebe, please chill for a bit. We have only just arrived. Allow us to rest.

Chima: While we are doing that, I shall use the interlude to rehabilitate my health. *(Fishes a pre-rolled Indian hemp and a gas lighter from his pocket)* Anyone care to share with me?

AKPOBI: Old man, so you haven't given that up?

AMADI: What the hell? Chima still smokes India hemp?

OSADEBE: Abeg make una leave Chima alone to take his self-medication jare.

CHIMA: Yes O! This is medicine for rheumatism. I take it for my joint pains. *(Lights up and begins to smoke)* Do you care for a drag Ben?

BEN LOCO: No thank you. I'd rather stick to my mentholated cigarettes.

CHIMA: This is definitely healthier than tobacco and snuff. The buds are purely organic. Hemp placates rheumatism you know. *(Puffs on the joint)*

AMADI: When did Indian hemp become a remedy for rheumatism?

CHIMA: Since the days of John the Baptist.

AMADI: What are you saying?

CHIMA: The Nazarene prophets who sojourned in the wilderness in the time of John the Baptist perceived hemp plant elevated their spirits during meditation. The Rastafarians later picked up on it and started using it to inspire their inner mind. However, the Indians later discovered that it could alleviate joint pains and started growing it for that purpose. That's why it is called rheumatism weed. Though many people smoke it to get high, it doesn't get me high at all. It just relieves my pain. *(Draws on the joint and blows out a stream of vapours)*

AMADI: *(Looks at Chima in disbelief)* That's absolute nonsense!

CHIMA: *(Shrugs)* Don't believe me if you won't.

AKPOBI: Where do you have your joint pain, Pa Chima?

CHIMA: On this leg *(Lifts his trousers and shows his left ankle)*.

AKPOBI: Hmm… Your ankle looks okay to me. You don't limp or anything like that. I thought the rheumatism was what caused your hunch back.

CHIMA: Rheumatism doesn't go above the waist.

AKPOBI: That's not true.

CHIMA: I am the one to tell you. You don't know any better.

AKPOBI: Of cores I do. Rheumatism can even affect the neck joint.

CHIMA: That's incorrect. Don't argue with me. I had already spent six years in this world eating my mother's cassava before you were even born.

AKPOBI: I think that grass you are smoking is beginning to affect your brain. Very soon, you will start hearing Bob Marley's lyrics and Sly Dunbar's rub-a-dub inside your head. Only a few seconds remain now before you get on your feet and start skanking.

[*The other comrades burst out laughing at Akpobi's jest. Chima scowls at them and smokes his weed*]

OSADEBE: *(Cuts in)* Enough of that now. Comrades, let's get serious. Nobody should crack any more jokes. If you don't have what better to say, simply stay quiet and reflect on the memories of your soldier life.

[*Osadebe fixes a stern look on the comrades. They fell quiet, then Osadebe droops his head and drifts into reminiscence. The others follow his example, each drifting into his own reverie. After a while, Akpobi quietly gets to his feet. He walks to the block platform, mounts it and bawls*]

AKPOBI: I, Captain Armstrong Akpobi retired, this day remembers when I was a soldier. As a young chap, rugged and full of valour, I enlisted into the 36 Division Infantry Battalion of Nigerian Army. During the colonial days, I was conscripted into the Commonwealth Allied Forces and trained by the European commanders to be a die-hard ranger. After that, we were brainwashed and bundled away to faraway Asia to fight against the Japanese and Indian armies in a war we had no business in! Comrades, do you remember that war?

COMRADES: *(Spring to their feet and shout)* Burma war!!!

AKPOBI: Yes, comrades, we were shipped there to fight. Those we fought against didn't offend our country in any way. Our colonial masters used us as puns in their own wars. We are lucky we survived and came back to tell the tale of the war. We all have our personal experiences. The battle in Burma was a suicide mission. We managed to escape all the waylays and traps the Asian soldiers put in our way.

OSADEBE: Those Japanese soldiers were bad Machiavellians who had many snare tricks up their sleeves. Real evil geniuses for sure!

BIGLER: The squad Ben and I were in suffered much from the landmines they placed in our paths. The mines distributed instant death. It was touch-and-go!

BEN LOCO: Some of our men shattered to pieces in a flash and their shredded bodies scattered across the field. We were afraid to gather their dismembered bodies for burial for fear of stepping on a mine. It was heart-breaking for me to watch vultures feast on the remains of my compatriots. Once, I couldn't bear the sight and instinctively shot at the birds to scare them off. I got a stern rebuke from our commander for wasting bullets.

AMADI: Our squad was badly fated by their booby traps. They killed our men like a pandemic. Some of the precise traps killed instantly. The dodgy ones killed slowly.

CHIMA: Oh my God! Don't even remind me of those pitfalls!
They personified death!

AKPOBI: Indeed, the traps were harbingers of terrible pain. Those that didn't kill pronto, inflicted unbearable pain.

OSADEBE: How the Asian devil soldiers made those traps work to precision still baffles me. I witnessed how one string trap caught one of our soldiers by his leg and snagged him unto a hidden spear that pierced his heart. He was dead before we could rescue him

CHIMA: I myself almost met my fate when I nearly fell into a pitfall. God saved me that day.

OSADEBE: I saw it happen. You were lucky.

AKPOBI: I also witnessed it. You were very lucky indeed!

CHIMA: I thank Almighty God for saving me.

BIGLER: How did it happen?

CHIMA: The bad guys dug a hole in a pathway and covered the top with loose dry palm fronds. Unaware of the danger, I stepped on the booby trap with one leg and fell forward. Miraculously, My head and my other leg caught on the ground across the pit, and my hands instinctively spread out like a cross and anchored into the soil on either side of the hole. Thus my frame remained suspended above the hole.

AKPOBI: That was when we came to your rescue and pulled you to a safe ground. When we observed the hole, we discovered a cleverly crafted metal structure with long upward-tilting razor sharp knives was cemented to the base. The thing looked gruesomely wicked!

CHIMA: Had I fallen into the pit, my testicles would have been a perfect target for the waiting blades! Can you imagine that? How could a man be so heartless to set knives in a trap to burst another man's testicles?

AKPOBI: Not only your testicles Chima, you would have lost your life too. we would have applied mercy killing on you and finished you off, for your own good.

CHIMA: Oh yes! We often did that for those who were unlucky. When we rescued a wounded soldier who was in severe pains, he begged us to shoot him because the pain was unbearable. His passionate guttural pleas motivated us to carry out his euthanasia request, so he could die in peace and spare our ears his agonising cries.

AMADI: We were lucky we survived.

OSADEBE: The Almighty God spared our lives.

AKPOBI: Comrades, do you remember that song we use to sing at night when we felt homesick?

OSADEBE: We sang many songs in Burma. Which one are you referring to in particular?

AKPOBI: I am talking about the nostalgic song. Let me refresh your memory. *(Comes down from the block platform and sings hoarsely)*
> Oh my home!
> Oh my home!
> When shall I see my home!
> When shall I see my native land!
> I will never forget my home!

AMADI: Oh yes! I remember that song now. We were never allowed to sing it loudly in the camp because the oyinbo commander of my platoon said it was a sign of weakness. Whenever I was in low spirits, or felt nostalgic, I hummed it silently. At other times, I crooned it in quiet tones at night, provided the commander couldn't hear me.

CHIMA: Let us sing that song now comrades. Let's sing like brave fighting soldiers and be young again.

OSADEBE: We can sing to the glory of old age and to the memories of yester year.

AKPOBI: Good, comrades. I shall raise the song again then we will all sing it together. Ready? Three, two, one… Oh my—

COMRADES: *(Interrupt with a shout)* No, Akpobi, don't raise the song please!!!

[*Akpobi glares at them with an embarrassed face*]

OSADEBE: Akpobi, kindly let Amadi lead the song. He has a better singing voice.

AKPOBI: Was that why you all cut me off like that? Anyway, in the spirit of camaraderie, carry on, Amadi.

AMADI: Thank you Comrade Akpobi. Chaii! It's been a long time since I last sang the song O! No problem shah, I am sure I can still sing it well.

[Amadi *braces himself, takes in a deep breath and breathes out. He breathes in and out again and opens his mouth to sing but Chima abruptly jumps towards him and covers his mouth. Everyone looks surprised, especially Amadi who looks at Chima confusedly*]

CHIMA: Wait, Amadi! Don't raise the song yet. Comrades, may I suggest that we arrange ourselves in a circular file? That was how we did it in Burma when we were marching around a bonfire. Let us march round these blocks *(Points at the blocks they had sat on)*, as we sing, just like old times. *(Removes his palm from Amadi's mouth)* What do you say Amadi?

AMADI: *(Spits)* Don't you ever place your dirty palm over my mouth again!

CHIMA: Are you crazy, Amadi? I am trying to coordinate things here and you are insulting me?

AMADI: Why should you place your hand over my mouth? It stinks of weed. *(Spits again)*

OSADEBE: Stop the fracas now both of you. Calm down, Amadi. Chima didn't mean any offence. He has in fact, suggested a very good thing. I second his idea. Let's do as he said. Amadi, you can start that song after we have arranged ourselves.

[*The comrades arrange themselves in a ring-file. Amadi joins them and raises the song. They all sing and march round the blocks*]

COMRADES: *(Singing)*
  Oh my home!
  Oh my home!
  When shall I see my home!
  When shall I see my native land!
  I will never forget my home!
  I leave my mother, I leave my father!
  I leave them faraway!
  When shall I see my native land!
  I will never forget my home!

[*The comrades continue to sing and march. They soon sing-march themselves into a jolly frenzy, oblivious of any other movements around them. Tiko enters and goes to offload his belongings on the block platform. He sits there watching the comrades, nodding along to their jolly song. Then he gets up and carries a block from the pile. He positions the block on the ground close to the comrades, stands on it and bawls in military jargon]*

TIKO: Hey hooyah! Ye shah at heeya! Stand at aye atteeeeeen-tion!

[The comrades promptly obey and stand erect with arms at their sides and feet together. Tiko continues]

TIKO: Histula! Hooyah hey -yah-hoorah! Stand at aye eeeeease!

[The comrades now relax their legs and crossed their hands behind their backs]

TIKO: Hey rah legion brigade yah di-do! I salute you Mighty ex-pongos of crack battalions! Ye sha in esprit de corps stand in formation for de cadent commandant salute!

[The comrades promptly arrange themselves in a horizontal line and face Tiko]

TIKO: Hey yuh! Hey hurrah! Super-duper brigade hey yuh-la-hooyah! Ye shah heehya! Ye shah at hiya! Hey rah de oohey! Salute!

[The comrades raise their right palms to their tempos in salute to Tiko and he salutes them back]

TIKO: Hey hoorah! Agile combative action aye! Firearm demo hooyah!

[*The comrades immediately take different combative postures. Each of them demonstrates carrying their combat firearm and begins to mimic the sounds of shooting*]

AKPOBI: Rat-a-tat-tat- rat-a-tat-tat! AK-47 hooyah! Die-hard ranger!

BEN LOCO: Kra-krakra-kra-kra-krakra-kra! Pump action hooyah! No-retreat-no-surrender marksman!

OSADEBE: Tuah-tuah-tuah-tuah-tuah-tuah! Luger hooyah! Hit and run trooper!

CHIMA: Tuah kaboom! RPG hooyah! Collateral target destroyer!

BIGLER: Kablam- kablam- kablam- kablam- kablam-kablam-kablam! Revolver hooyah! Face-to-face daredevil!

AMADI: Pa-ta-pa-ta-pa-ta-pa-ta-pa-ta! Thompson submachine hooyah! Trigger happy commando!

TIKO: Kpoar! Kpoar! Kpoar! Aba-made pistol hooyah! Biafra guerrilla runs four-forty when MAC 10 clickety-click! Hey hoorah! Let's proceed to march drill lahoolah! Left-right! Left-right!

[*The comrades start to march on the spot, stomping their feet vigorously. Tiko continues the drills*]

TIKO: Left-right! Left-right! Left-right! Left-right! Now go! Forwaaaaaard march!

[*The comrades start marching forwards. Tiko raises a new song and marches behind them*]

COMRADES: *(All singing and marching along)*
    I remember when I was a soldier!
    I remember when I was a soldier!
    Hippie yah-yah hippie-hippie yah-yah!
    Hippie yah-yah hippie-hippie yah-yah!
    I remember when I was a soldier!
    I remember when I was a soldier!
    Hippie yah-yah hippie-hippie yah-yah!
    Hippie yah-yah hippie-hippie yah-yah!

[*Tiko raises another song and the comrades join in*]

TIKO: Soldier go come and soldier go go, but the barrack go always remain! If old soldier dies today he will die no more! left-right! left-right!

COMRADES: Forward ever, backward never! If I die today I will die no more!

TIKO: Soldier go come and soldier go go, but old soldier prayers go bring am back from war! Left-right! left-right!

COMRADES: Forward ever, backward never! If I die today I will die no more!

TIKO: Soldier go come and soldier go go, but old soldier guardian angel go protect am in war! Left-right! left-right!

COMRADES: Forward ever, backward never! If I die today I will die no more!

TIKO: Soldier go come and soldier go go, but old soldier combat skills go keep am alive in war! Left-right! left-right!

COMRADES: Forward ever, backward never! If I die today I will die no more!

TIKO: Soldier go come and soldier go go, but old soldier charm go make am invincible in war! Left-right! left-right!

COMRADES: Forward ever, backward never! If I die today I will die no more!

TIKO: Old soldier life na one life! Forward ever backward never!

COMRADES: Once a soldier, always a soldier! If I die today I will die no more!

TIKO: Old soldier way na one way! Forward ever backward never!

COMRADES: Once a soldier, always a soldier! If I die today I will die no more!

[*They carry on singing and proceed to march out of the scene*]

LIGHT FADES

Scene Five

[*The scene opens again on the same grass field. Six of the comrades (with the exception of Tiko) are there sitting on the cement blocks. Martial music plays in the background. The comrades sit in silence, each looking deep in thought. Tiko enters from behind. He stands and observes the comrades. The Music stops. He speaks*]

TIKO: Greetings, comrades!

COMRADES: Greetings Comrade Tiko!!!!!!

TIKO: Be not afraid. We are on track to march for a course that is our right! We have been waiting for the Government to pay us our pensions. We have waited, waited and waited to no avail. They have made us wait in vain! We are exhausted. Why are we being deprived of an enjoyable life in our old ages? What we really need is to be in our homes in the care of geriatric carers. But where is the money to employ them?

COMRADES: With our Government!!!!!!

TIKO: Where are our pensions, which we could have used to pay them?

COMRADES: With our Government!!!!!!

TIKO: We are entitled to our pensions. we are not supposed to be begging for what is ours. Unless we act now, we might all die and never get our money. Are we going to let that happen?

COMRADES: No O!!!!!!

TIKO: Precisely! We will wait no more! Those who aren't sure of what they want dream dreams. Those who are sure, have hopes. We were assured of our pensions, hence we were hopeful. But our Government have dashed our hopes and turned us to mere dreamers. Are we dreamers comrades?

COMRADES: No O!!!!!!

TIKO: Why should it be a problem for Government to pay us our pensions?

COMRADES: We wonder!!!!!!

TIKO: Now that we wish to air our grievances, who should take the blame?

COMRADES: Our government!!!!!!

TIKO: As agreed, our march will be on Remembrance Day. The same day they will pay respect to the fallen comrades Who don't benefit from the memorial. It would've been great if our government looked after the survivors rather than waste our country's money on singing the praises of the dead. We are no fools, comrades. Enough is enough!

COMRADES: Enough is enough!!!!!!

TIKO: We are going to demand for what is rightfully ours!

COMRADES: Yes, our pensions are our right!!!!!!

TIKO: Good. Comrades, let's rehearse for tomorrow. Our march at the parade grounds should be on point. Are you ready?

COMRADES: We are more than ready!!!!!!

TIKO: Good! First of all, as patriots, we must be patriotic to our Mother Land. So, before anything else, let us sing our National Anthem. Stand, all of you. Let' us sing!

[*The comrades stand and wait for Tiko to lead the anthem*]

TIKO: Arise O compatriots, Nigeria's call obey. To serve our father land. With love and strength and…

[*Tiko breaks off because he is the only one singing. He looks at the comrades questioningly. They stare back at him defiantly*]

TIKO: Why are you not singing, comrades?

[*The comrades do not answer*]
TIKO: What's the matter?

[*Silence*]

TIKO: Comrades?

[*The comrades remain silent*]

TIKO: What's wrong? Why are you quiet?

[*The silent comrades continue to stare Tiko down. Tiko is confused*]

TIKO: Why are you looking at me like that? Can you talk to me please.

COMRADES: We don't know the words of that anthem!!!!!!

TIKO: Seriously? You mean you can't sing our National Anthem?

COMRADES: We know the other one!!!!!!

TIKO: What do you mean?

AKPOBI: Look Tiko, The anthem you sang is the new one. It is not the one we learnt. all of us here retired from the force before our National Anthem was changed.

BIGLER: Don't think you are better than us because you can sing it!

BEN LOCO: You were only privileged to learn the new anthem because our government changed it before you retired.

TIKO: Comrades, let's not quarrel. I accept that I was privileged, so let's move on from that. But we have to sing our National Anthem. I will have to teach you the words so you can learn it. Is that okay?

AKPOBI: I don't wish to learn the anthem.

TIKO: Are you serious?

AKPOBI: I am dead serious! I didn't come all the way from my home to learn the national anthem.

TIKO: Please Comrade Akpobi, listen—

AKPOBI: No, you listen. I am not interested, period!

TIKO: *(Turns to the others)* Please comrades, talk to him.

COMRADES: We are with Akpobi!!!!!

TIKO: What?

COMRADES: We don't wish to learn the anthem!!!!!

TIKO: Are you serious?

COMRADES: We are dead serious. We are not interested, period!!!!!

TIKO: *(looking from one to the other)* But comrades, It's important that we sing our national anthem before anything else. you have to learn it. Let me teach you the words.

BIGLER: To hell with the anthem!

CHIMA: Light it in flames!

OSADEBE: Let fire betide it!

BEN LOCO: Shoot it with a blunderbuss!

AMADI: Blast it with a grenade!

AKPOBI: Destroy it with a bazooka!

TIKO: *(Looks at them in disbelief)* You all can't be serious.

BEN LOCO: The old anthem is better. Let us sing that one.

BIGLER: I prefer that one too. It's the one the oyinbo woman composed for our country. I think she was either Mungo Park's or Lord Lugard's wife or so.

BEN LOCO: Don't say what you don't know Bigler. Do you even know the year Lord Lugard came to our country, let alone the year Mungo Park was here.

BIGLER: Here Ben Loco O? So you want to teach me history now or what?

BEN LOCO: I will teach you what you don't know since you are so daft to think the oyinbo woman was the wife of Mungo Park.

BIGLER: I said it was either him or Lord Lugard's, not so?

BEN LOCO: For your information, the oyinbo woman's name was Mary Slessor.

BIGLER: Thank you for telling me her name, but whose wife was she then? Or you don't know?

BEN LOCO: She was the wife of Mungo Park. Your second guess was right.

TIKO: You old men should stop saying what you don't know. The oyinbo woman was not called Mary Slessor, nor was she Mungo Park's wife.

CHIMA: I remember Lord Lugard's wife was called Flora Shaw. Was that her name?

TIKO: Far from it. Her name was Lillian Jean Williams.

BIGLER: Thank you Tiko for supplying the answer. You are the bookish one. but whose wife was she?

TIKO: I don't think she married. But Let's leave that matter alone and focus on singing the anthem.

OSADEBE: I remember we used to sing the old anthem with lots of enthusiasm. Things were still good in our country then.

AKPOBI: The old anthem was a true unity song that made me feel proud of my country. I would hold our flag and stand at attention like a green-and-white dinosaur as I sang it.

CHIMA: The anthem bound us together as compatriots, though we scatter across the country in geographical zones with different mother tongues.

TIKO: Honestly, the old National Anthem was the best one for our people. The lyrics were really good. I wonder why they had to scrap it.

CHIMA: Let me enlighten you, Tiko. Our government are artful changers. They changed the anthem like they changed everything else in our country.

TIKO: *(Nodding)* You' got it right of course! Our government are very skilled in changing things from good to worse.

CHIMA: That's absolutely true! Everything our government does seems like moving things from the frying pan to fire.

TIKO: They are inconsistent. Nothing they do remains the same for long.

CHIMA: Exactly! Since after our independence, our government has been consistent in the manner they changed things around in our country. Let me count some of their chameleonic changes for you. When I ask a question, if you know the answer, chorus it. Number one, who changed our driving from right-hand drive to left-hand drive?

COMRADES: Our government!!!!!!

CHIMA: Who changed our currency from Pound Sterling and Pence to Naira and Kobo?

COMRADES: Our government!!!!!!

CHIMA: Who made our country change from refining and exporting petrol to importing it from abroad?

COMRADES: Our government!!!!!!

CHIMA: Who privatised NITEL, NEPA and limited our NNPC?

COMRADES: Our government!!!!!!

CHIMA: Who introduced larger naira denominations and withdrew the lower denominations from circulation?

COMRADES: Our government!!!!!!

CHIMA: Who made sure nothing in the economy is sold in kobo anymore and encouraged the banks not to pay out the kobo balances in our bank accounts?

COMRADES: Our government!

CHIMA: Who deregulated our domestic currency to make their dollars stashed in foreign banks more powerful than the naira?

COMRADES: Our government!!!!!!

CHIMA: Who passed bills to increase their own allowances in preference to bills that increase gross domestic products?

COMRADES: Our government!!!!!!

CHIMA: Who don't pay public workers' salaries regularly?

COMRADES: Our government!!!!!!

CHIMA: Also, who don't want to pay old soldiers their pensions?

COMRADES: Our government!!!!!!

CHIMA: I rest my case. We have said it all. You may carry on, Tiko.

TIKO: *(Taking over)*, Our pensions are our main concern. we do not mind all the conjures of our government. We need are daily bread. what is ours is ours! We need our money before the Pension officials pay it all to unknown pensioners. Rise now comrades. Let us sing the old National Anthem to remind ourselves of when we were agile and young.

That time when things were still good in our country… when our dustbins used to have leftover food and our dogs didn't have to go about eating excrement because they had fed well. Let's sing, then we can practise our march. Tomorrow is the D-day. We will need to rest after, so comrades, oya, get up, arrange yourselves now. Let's do it sharp-sharp!

[*The comrades get on their feet, some pump their fists into the air excitedly. They form two rows, three stand in front of three. They stand at attention and look at Tiko*]

TIKO: comrade Amadi, raise the anthem for us please.

[*Amadi raises the song. The comrades sing*]

Nigeria we hail thee
Our own dear native land
Though tribe and tongue may differ
In brotherhood we stand
Nigerians all are proud to serve
Our sovereign mother land…

Our flag shall be a symbol that truth and justice reign,
In peace or battle honoured, and this we count as gain,
To hand on to our children a banner without stain.

O God of all creation, grant this our one request:
Help us to build a nation where no man is oppressed,
And so with peace and plenty Nigeria may be blessed.

[T*he comrades finish singing the anthem and place their right palms on their chests. They recite the National Pledge, then Tiko raises a song and they all sing*]

We are marching on a sunrise day!
It is a day for us to rise and march to victory!
We are marching on our way it's a lovely day today!
Marching on a sunrise day!
We are marching on a sunrise day!
It is a day for us to rise and march to victory!
We are marching on our way it's a lovely day today!
Marching on a sunrise day!

[*The comrades sing the song repeatedly and proceed to march off the stage*]

LIGHT FADES

Scene Six

[*The scene opens on the Arcade grounds where the Armed Forces Remembrance Day celebration is ongoing. A military percussion sestet plays a rendition in an attenuated volume. Not far from the performing band is a cenotaph where the monument of a sculptured soldier stands with three separate flagpoles that hoist the flags of the army, navy and air force.*

Two canopies (one popular and one state) are set on one side in an L-shape arrangement with some rows of chairs. At the front of the central chairs in the state canopy is a large rectangular head-table which is laid over with a sparkly white cloth. A line of green-white-green buntings is used to decorate the front of the table. The table is also decorated with flowers-filled vases that are blazoned with the coat of arms. Also on the table are light refreshment and programme booklets. The floor under the table is covered with a red carpet which forms a path to the right flank, where seven ceremonially dressed armed guards of honour (two air force, two navy and three army, one of which is Opara, Osadebe's son) are standing in exhibition. The guards hold their rifles by the muzzles beside them with the butts resting on the ground.

Standing with his back to the guards and facing the state canopy in a ceremonial outfit and white gloves is the guards' commander who holds a long tapered sword by the hilt in his right hand. The president and other dignitaries sit in the state canopy including the Vice president, the Minister of Defence, the four service chiefs comprising the bosses of the air force, army, navy and defence staff.

Also present, is an Imam, a Catholic priest, a Protestant clergy, the senate president, the speaker of the house of reps, other who is who of the executive council, some foreign invitees and the other guests in the popular canopy.

Keeping guard at the positions of the four cardinal points are baton-bearing police officers. A separate police officer who is wearing a superintendent's badge stands close to the state canopy.

The military band renders the National Anthem, after which the imam and the clergies make the opening prayers. Then the commander of the guards brigade addresses the state canopy]

COMMANDANT: Your Excellency! Chiefs of Staff! Lords Temporal, other protocols duly and respectfully observed. I, Captain Hassan Kanji, Commander of Guards Brigade for this august occasion, hereby announce the commencement of the clarion call reveille to kick off today's Armed Forces Remembrance Day' Ceremony. The bugle will now be sounded to summon the souls of the fateful departed soldiers to the cenotaph.

[*The sound of the bugle promptly wafts into the arena and carries on for a few minutes before it ends. Then the commander speaks*]

COMMANDANT: Your Excellency Sir, The souls of the departed heroes have been duly summoned and are here present with us by the cenotaph. I will now prepare the guards of honour for inspection! (T*urns to the ceremonial soldiers and bawls in military jargon)*

[*The ceremonial soldiers raise their right legs, stamp them on the ground and stand at attention*]

COMMANDANT: Your Excellency and chiefs of Staff! The Guards of Honour are ready for inspection!

[*The president, the minister of defence and the four army bosses rise from their chairs. They walk along the red carpet towards the commandant and he leads them on a walk round the ceremonial guards. They complete the inspection and the president and his entourage go back to their seats. The Commandant carries on officiating*]

COMMANDANT: Your Excellency Sir! We shall shortly proceed to grace this occasion with the laying of wreaths on the cenotaph in honour of the fallen heroes. Then we will take the march past from the regiments and other representatives. Thereafter the guards in view will perform the customary volley of live rounds to honour the fallen heroes with 21-gun salute. Before we proceed further, let us first observe a minute of silence for the souls of the fateful departed heroes. Please rise to your feet as a mark of respect.

[*Everyone stands. After a minute of silence, a gunshot suddenly rends the air to mark the end of the moment. The guests sit down*]

COMMANDANT: Your Excellency, it is time for the laying of wreaths on the cenotaph.

[*The military band starts to play. The president and the service chiefs rise to their feet. With his Excellency at the lead, they walk with slow, solemn movements to the cenotaph and each of them places a wreathe by the tomb post. After they return to their seats, other dignitaries including the representatives of the legion and the widows of the fallen heroes also go to lay a wreath and go back to sit. The band stops playing*]

COMMANDANT: Your Excellency Sir! We will now observe the march past parades from the regiments and other associations who are waiting in the wings. Permit me your Excellency to introduce the first regiment to start the march past. I call on the—

[*The Commandant suddenly breaks off at the sound of an approaching boisterous singing and turns to look. Advancing from the main entrance of the arena, in two-row formation of three men in a line, the ex-service soldiers, all dressed in their former military regalia's and garrison caps march towards the centre. Tiko follows behind leading the song. Everyone fixes their eyes on them*]

TIKO: Zombie way na one way!

COMRADES: A joro jara joro!!!!!!

TIKO: Zombie way na one way!

COMRADES: A joro jara joro!!!!!!

TIKO: No break no gear no stop!

COMRADES: A joro jara joro!!!!!!

TIKO: Soldier life na one life!

COMRADES: A joro jara joro!!!!!!

TIKO: His life get two options!

COMRADES: A joro jara joro!!!!!!

TIKO: Option one na death!

COMRADES: A joro jara joro!!!!!!

TIKO: Option two na to survive!

COMRADES: A joro jara joro!!!!!!

TIKO: No brake no gear no stop!

COMRADES: A joro jara joro!!!!!!

[*They end the song and Tiko immediately starts another*]

TIKO: Na who dem dey remember?

COMRADES: Na soldier wey don die!!!!!!

TIKO: Who dem dey honour?

COMRADES: Na dead soldiers wey no dey here!!!!!!

TIKO: Who dem dey blow trumpet for?

COMRADES: Na dead soldiers wey no fit hear anything!!!!!!

TIKO: Who dem dey parade for?

COMRADES: Na dead soldiers wey no fit see anything!!!!!!

TIKO: Who dem dey lay flowers for?

COMRADES: na dead soldiers wey no fit appreciate anything!!!!!!

TIKO: Who dem dey lavish our money on?

COMRADES: Na dead soldiers wey no need am!!!!!!

TIKO: So who really needs the money?
COMRADES: Na the living old soldiers!!!!!!

TIKO: The living old soldiers are here now!

COMRADES: We are the living old soldiers!!!!!!

TIKO: Old soldiers with no money!

COMRADES: We are the moneyless old soldiers!!!!!!

TIKO: Old soldiers who are hungry!

COMRADES: We are the hungry old soldiers!!!!!!

TIKO: Old soldiers who are angry!

COMRADES: We are the angry old soldiers!!!!!!

TIKO: The old soldiers need their pensions!

COMRADES: We want our money Mr President!!!!!!

TIKO: The old soldiers want their pensions!

COMRADES: We need our money Mr President!!!!!!

[*The comrades have reached the centre of the arena by now. Tiko suddenly bawls*]

TIKO: Hey hooyah! Ye shah at heeya! Stand at aye atteeeeeen-tion!

[*The comrades stamp their feet, keep their legs together with their hands at their sides and remain still. Tiko continues*]

TIKO: Histula! Hooyah hey -yah-hoorah! Stand at aye eeeeease!

[*The comrades simultaneously stand with their legs relaxed and their hands crossed behind their backs*]

TIKO: I salute ye mighty ex-service combatants! Hey yuh-la-hooyah! We my higher ex-pongos of crack battalions will in esprit de corps stand to pay respect to our fallen pongos!

[*The comrades and Tiko promptly arrange themselves in a horizontal line and face the cenotaph. They observe a moment of silence then Tiko carries on*]

TIKO: Hey yuh hurrah! Super-duper commandoes! wee shah yuh-la-hooyah heigh ho salute the Commander-in-chief!

[*The comrades and Tiko turn to face the state canopy raising their right palms to their tempos in salute to the president. At this juncture, the policemen and the superintendent leave their spots and advance towards them. Everyone else begins to talk among themselves, with the exception of the ceremonial guards of honour and the Commandant who remain watching like statues. The President talks hurriedly to the Minister of Defence who is nodding to everything he is saying. The policemen, with the superintendent at the front, stand in a horizontal line and form a cordon before the comrades. Then the superintendent snaps at the comrades*]

SUPERINTENDENT: In the name of the law, I order you to disband and disperse from here at once!

TIKO: Stand back, Oga policeman. Give us a chance. This matter does not concern you.

SUPERINTENDENT: I say clear off from here now all of you!

TIKO: Who do you think you are talking to? Do you think you are speaking to your junior officers? Refrain from addressing us in your pompous language.

SUPERINTENDENT: In the name of the law and in the interest of national security, leave this arena at once!

TIKO: Don't shout at us my friend! Who do you think you are? A common police SP like you? Look, let me tell you, I and these men *(Points at the comrades)* had ranks way higher than yours before we retired from the army. Be mindful of how you talk to us! *(Flicks a warning finger at the Superintendent)*

SUPERINTENDENT: *(Steps forward)* I will not repeat myself after this. For the last time, I say disband and disperse from this arena right now! Vamoose now!

[*The comrades burst into a scornful laugh. Tiko holds up a hand to stop them*]

TIKO: You are very rude. You dress like a police superintendent, but barks like a police dog. We do not have time for your woofs. Give way for us to address the president.

SUPERINTENDENT: (*Now angry*) Alright! Move back, move off all of you!

TIKO: We are not leaving here if Mr President doesn't address us.

SUPERINTENDENT: My friend move or I will move you! *(Pushes Tiko who falls)*

TIKO: *(Gets up, stands a few centimetres away from the superintendent's and sticks a finger in his face)* You pushed a man who's old enough to be your father? How dare you? You are a disgrace to our culture! Is that how they treat old men in your place? If you dare lay your filthy hand on me again, I will show you that I am an old soldier!

[*The superintendent hits his baton on Tiko's knee. Tiko falls and pines in pain on the ground. Akpobi steps forward, yanks the baton off the Superintendent's hand and hits him on the head with it. The superintendent lands on his buttocks and holds his head as blood drips through his fingers from a cut. The other policemen rush at Akpobi and clobber him with their batons. The comrades descend upon the policemen and a fight starts between the lot.*

The fighting snowballs a stampede in the arena and people take to their heels using the closest exit. Opara remains and goes to beat the policemen his father is fighting with.

The group fight continues. Finally, the policemen give up and take to their heels. The comrades and Opara pursue them around the arena in a mock fashion. The policemen try to escape through the exit in the left wing but Opara's colleagues suddenly emerge in their way pointing their rifles. The policemen detour and flee through the central aisle out of the arena. Opara re-joins his colleagues and they exit.

The comrades are battered, having bruises and looking solemn. They gather some scattered chairs together and sit, casting their faces downwards. BIGLER grunts like a wounded lion. Amadi sneezes and fishes out his snuffbox. He helps himself to some snuff before passing the snuffbox to Osadebe, who also snorts some. Ben Loco fishes out his packet of Marlborough and finds it empty when he opens it. He crumples the pack and flings it away angrily, then he begins to hum the nostalgic song in a sad tone. The others join in one after the other, humming in tandem and mimicking Ben's tone]

CHIMA: *(Stops suddenly and holds his ribcage, wincing in pain)* I feel a terrible pain here.

[*The comrades stop and look at Chima*]

AKPOBI: Are you sure, Pa Chima?

CHIMA: *(Winces more fretfully, still clasping his side)* I might have sustained an internal injury. I think I have a broken rib.

AMADI: Tufiakwa, God will not let that happen to you Chima!

OSADEBE: Lie down Chima and let me check it for you.

BEN LOCO: It's better he remains in a sitting position. He will feel less pain that way.

BIGLER: *(Moving to Chima)* Let me do it for him, Osadebe. *I am good at resetting bones. Try to relax Chima.* I will take your uniform off and see what's going on there.

[*Suddenly, Chima drops to the ground and starts growling like a dying animal. Bigler rushes to him and props him into a sitting position. The other comrades gather around them in confusion. Bigler quickly unbuttons Chima's jacket but stops short when Chima starts to cough up blood! The comrades are horrified. Chima suddenly slumps and stretches out on the ground before they could get over their surprise. OSADEBE rushes over and places his ear on Chima's chest. He lifts Chima's hand and it drops limply. He screams*]

OSADEBE: No! No-no-no! Chima don't go!

[*Osadebe continues to shake Chima's body and laments. Realisation dawn on the other comrades. They begin to weep in tandem. Ben Loco and Bigler pound on Chima's body to rouse him, but Chima is no longer with them. The comrades lift Chima's corpse up like a coffin. They carry their dead comrade out of the arena, mourning bitterly as they go*]

LIGHT FADES

THE END

Glossary

A

agbada: an extravagantly tailored three-piece traditional men's attire.

abeg: please (Nigerian pidgin)

Ama Ijiji: an imaginary village (literally means hamlet of flies).

aside: a line spoken by an actor to the audience but not intended for others on the scene.

A joro jara joro: a chorus excerpt adapted from Fela Kuti zombie lyrics

ASUU: Academic Staff Union of Universities.

ASUP: Academic Staff Union of Polytechnics.

Aba-made: a firearm that was manufactured in Aba during the Nigeria Civil War.

B

bloodshot: red.

bellicose: Having or showing a ready disposition to fight.

boorish: Ill-mannered.

buntings: small triangular flags.

Biafra: the republic which tried to break out of Nigeria during the Civil War.

booby trap: a hidden trap or bomb that is set along a walk path.

bugle: a loud-sounding trumpet used by the military.

blunderbuss: a short gun with a wide muzzle.

C

camaraderie: the spirit of trust and loyalty among people.

Chineke-meh: my God (Igbo language).

Chaii: an Exclamation expressing surprise, or hesitation (Igbo language).

cordon: a line of police officers that forms a barricade.

cenotaph: a monument built in honour of a dead person.

cigarillo: small cigar or cigarette wrapped in tobacco instead of paper.

communiqué: a press release.

D
detour: taking another route due to obstacle.
diplococci: an infection that attacks the respiratory tract which can cause coughing.
dem: they (Nigeria pidgin)
dey: is/are (Nigeria Pidgin)

E
euthanasia: killing someone at their own request.
esprit de corps: the spirit of a group that makes the members want the group to succeed.

F
FCT: Federal Capital Territory of Nigeria.
fit: can't (Nigeria pidgin)

G
gaga: crazy
go go: will go (Nigeria pidgin)
Ghana-must-go bag: a cheap durable synthetic carryall bag (Nigerian pidgin).
gragra: violence (Nigerian pidgin).
geriatric: the treatment and care for old people.
gargoyle: an ugly fretwork hung on roofs to direct the flow of rain water.
Goat has eaten palm leaf off my head: an exclamation of perplex which is a literal translation of 'ewu atam igu na isi' (Igbo language).

H
hilt: the handle of a sword.
haba: what? (Nigerian pidgin, derived from Hausa).

J
jare: please (Nigerian pidgin)
jerkin: a sleeveless jacket.
jackass: a stupid fool.

K

kaii: an Exclamation expressing surprise or hesitation (Hausa language).

L

legion: a group of ex-servicemen

landmine: an explosive hidden in the ground that sets off when stepped on.

M

marigold: bright yellow or orange colour.

martial music: military music.

N

NUPENG: Nigeria Union of Petroleum and Natural Gas Workers

NITEL: Nigeria Telecommunication Limited.

NEPA: National Electricity Power Authority.

NNPC: Nigeria National Petroleum Corporation.

na: is/the (Nigerian pidgin)

O

opata: nonsense (Nigerian pidgin)

odeshi: a protective charm against death (Igbo language).

okporoko: a stock fish (Nigerian pidgin).

Oga: Mister (Nigerian pidgin).

oya: quickly (Nigerian pidgin).

Oyinbo: a name for a white person (Nigerian pidgin).

Oghene biko: God please (Urhobo language).

P

prodigal: wasteful.

platoon: an army unit under the command of a lieutenant.

pongo: an enlisted person who serves in an army.

R

ranger: a member of a military unit trained for hit-and-run raids.

razmataz: showy or exciting display

regalia: a fine or decorative clothing worn in ceremonies.

runs four-forty: runs away fast (Nigerian pidgin).

S
strife: a disagreement or conflict.
silhouette: a dark outline of an object.
Scandinavia: the colder regions in Europe.
shah: anyway (Nigeria pidgin)
sestet: Six performers who perform together
somniloquism: talking while asleep.
super-duper: excellent.
supine: lying on ones back while facing upwards.

T
thermal: designed to retain heat.
Tufiakwa: God forbids (Igbo language)

W
wing: the side area on a stage where characters exit.
Wallahi: I swear to God (Nigerian pidgin, derived from Arabic).
wey: that
Y
yamutu: die (Nigerian pidgin).

www.ingramcontent.com/pod-product-compliance
Lightning Source LLC
Chambersburg PA
CBHW060344050426
42449CB00011B/2818